Contemporary Bestiary

Vasilina Orlova

Contemporary Bestiary

Copyright © 2014 Vasilina Orlova.

All rights reserved. No part of this book may be reproduced or transmitted in any form or by any means whatsoever without permission from the author, except in the case of brief quotations embodied in articles and reviews.

ISBN 978-0-9916009-0-8

First Edition

Gutenberg Printing Press Independent Group, Austin

Cover art and illustrations by Evellean

Photo by Katya Tavrizyan

Contents

American Road

    Blast 3

    American Road (I) 4

    Apparition 7

    Memoir 8

    Elgin Courier 10

    Birth 12

    Files 13

    Mother 14

    Corridor 16

    Tent 17

    Library 18

    American Road (II) 20

    Pick You Up 22

    Beads 24

    Arts 25

    El Paso 26

Lancaster	28
ID	31
What Time Is It?	32
Coca-Cola	33
Conditioners	34
Utopia	35
Whitman	36
The Best Cigars	40
Amanda	42
Odysseus	43
Clothespin	46
The Communist Party of the Soviet Union	48

A Variety of Dragons

Station	51
Moscow	54
Tattoo	58
Hairdo	60
Scarf	62
Kiev Kitchen	65

Siberian Dream	66
Story	67
Assignment	68
My Aunt's Ear Clips	70
The Lake	72
Library	74
Incantation	77
Cigarette	80
An Ability to Speak	82

Brilliant Robots

Borges	87
Limbo	88
After the Rain	89
Buddha	90
Home	91
Lipstick	92
Sect	93
Machaon	94
Count Leo Tolstoy's Estate	95

A Purple and Gray Umbrella 96

1941 97

Porn 98

Ataraxy 99

Landscape 100

Smoker 101

Pretext 102

Shih Tzu 103

9/11 104

Ghost of a Bicycle 105

Untitled 108

Cat 109

R705QS 110

Farewell 112

Apocalypse of Suburbia

Undo 115

Buoy 116

Preferences 117

Wife 118

A Great Shot	119
A Photo Not Taken	120
Thing	122
Neck	123
Photo	124
Fountain	126
Waterfall	127
San Antonio	128
Order	130
Map	131
Apocalypse of Suburbia	132
A Unicorn, a Dandelion, and a Lion	134

Self-Loading Parrots

Shield	137
Marketplace	138
Pendulum	140
Letter	142
Room	143
Dream	144

Fish	147
Falling	148
Letters to Several Personages.	
To Mr. Christopher Brooke	150
Wriggle	153
Stanzas	154
Phantasm of a Bicycle	156
Robotic Paradise	157
Bird	160
A Visitor	164
Ribs	166
Difference	167
Words	168
Insomniac	169
Gmail	170
Shorter	171
Message	172
Hotel Room	176
Evidence	178
Flip	179

Blast

An envoy of the north is in civilian dress,

Incognito and recognized by no one

He drives into the city,

Wheels tearing space.

He inquires where the short cut is

Through this rustic town with an urban heart,

And a peasant with some pheasants

Acknowledges him as a compatriot.

This pleasant country is damned full of strangers.

But looking at the smoke of the speeding car,

He suddenly remembers

Where he heard the accent.

The horizon

Is a sea of flame.

American Road (I)

The smoothness of American roads is entertaining
                               and nostalgic,
it evokes the images of sole wagon and cowboys
cinematically replicated in an endless succession of
    billboards, road signs, fast food eateries,
    filling stations, churches and ranches,
    channels and cactuses.

When you glide down this road—
wide, with as many lanes as are needed for a particular
location, marked with white and yellow lines,
you spot a dead armadillo or something else,
sometimes a deer;
a skinless former creature, a flick of the color
        and texture of fresh meat in a supermarket,
or else you see an aluminum mailbox
                               with a knob-lever,

with numbers,

with worn-out stripes and stars (painted).

The landscape exists insomuch as the road exists. Its constant unrolling presence is a sequence of rapidly changing scenery but there is a primal continuity—the road itself.

It mesmerizes a driver like a kaleidoscope

in which she sees her birth,

life,

and death.

As if in a gondola you slide by its mirror-like surface in a car, switching places but still not even for a moment leaving the ultimate territory of your lulling solitude.

You should tape it all, along with the music playing, to be able to recreate it in all its minute but important features in some other place, about as stable and devoid of movement as is possible for places, maybe under the earth.

It looks like a video game created by an almighty computer with the infernal ability to render the landscapes and vistas in millions of precise and multifaceted details.

And this is the embodied utopia of a state presenting itself in an unending landscape.

When I cross the inevitability of it,

it'll be

just

for

fun.

Apparition

The moment I saw you

I saw the black Moscow street behind you

Somehow I don't know why

Despite your funny round-eyed Studebaker.

After the rain

The lollipop

Lay like a dead sea fish

On the grainy tarmac of the parking lot

Adding a wave of yellow

To the rainbow stain of gasoline.

Memoir

We met in Paris

An amanuensis

The music sounded in the cafe

Diminuendo

She had long nails

And the smallest hat

I'd ever seen.

She was around

Ten years

Older than I was

She must be old now

If not dead

A pair of such thin legs

An amanuensis

With long curled black hair,

Pharaonic eyes

As if in Memphis

Not in Paris

She must be dead now

Never after

Did I see a woman

With such a small hat.

Elgin Courier

In the middle of the day the windows of Elgin Courier

Are blind with the sun and dust

A boy who comes into the room

In which the clack of typewriters are scattered,

The son of a journalist

Stands still

Twiddling a button of his shirt

And finally forgetting it

He looks at the blinkingly bald editor

                               with a pipe between his teeth

Who glances through the freshly printed pages

Either frowning and smiling

Or smiling and humming under his breath.

In the smoke shredded by the lamp

                               under green fringed cover

The big clock in the corner

And the glass *presse-papier*

                      on the green broadcloth of the table

Are as evidently present but unclear

As the almost lightless sleeping town in the windows.

Birth

She is like fifteen years younger than me

It's like

I was, you know, playing a computer game

On my first computer

When she followed her path

Head first

Between her exhausted mother's thighs.

Files

I guess maybe I should now

Divide the folder *Russia* on my computer

Into two,

And rename one of them *USA*,

And folder *USA*

Rename to, simply, *Files*, or *2013*,

For my life turned into the archive

And my occasional files

Turned out to be the traces

Of my current life

About

As real as it gets.

Mother

That evening

I was repeatedly raped

And sodomized

I had bruises

I had a cut on my mouth

Right here

And was left lying

On a concrete floor

For some minutes

Maybe hours

When my mother was dying

In the hospital,

She raised her clenched fist,

She said:

Jennifer!

I am very angry,

Jennifer.

It should have been me,

Not you,

Jennifer.

I am your mother.

I should have protected you.

I took her arm in mine.

Corridor

She is calm, forty, frowning, and not in a hurry,

Stuck at a station between trains

Without an exit.

She caught a cold, and now is sick,

Sick and traveling,

And the empty corridor of a hospital

Is what is waiting.

Behind the wall

A distant relative

Is grudgingly dying,

He is attached to an IV

With life-suspending liquid.

She is sick, patient, and is reading

A small, black book in a soft cover.

A ray of a lamp is oblique

And flickering.

It will soon be over.

Tent

Under the bright sun

My hair is whitened

My T-shirt bleached

Open skin tanned,

And my boy's arms and neck

Are gilded.

Everything is tempered.

The city is a tempera,

Temporarily scissored out of the course

Of evening events.

Even the chairs are attenuated,

They are withdrawing

In the constantly diminishing stripe of shadow,

Projected by a tent.

Library

Look at these children

Who are probably not done

With their final exams yet.

They sit

At the table in the library,

Two belated learners,

Beastly tired each,

Leaning

Above the ancient treatise,

Rubbing their red eyes,

As if in the warm odor of sinking flowers.

Their heads fall down on their hands.

In a crystal sphere nothing is seen

But a cloud and a crevice.

They start to suspect,

Or better let us say,

They always had a clear understanding,

And only hoped

That this is not so:

Time flows like speech,

By means of speech it flows.

In the hour-glass of the city

The quiet sand purls

Swallow

Outside the high windows,

The willow creaks.

American Road (II)

The hills and fields

Unrolling a way

My eye

Could not get used to seeing—

Unknown,

And yet vaguely familiar,

Strangely remind me

The fields where a rider,

Wounded by an arrow of Mongolian origin,

Was jolted

On his stumbling horse.

He dismounted,

He lay down next to the stone,

Listening for the fading

Raven cry and Kurt Cobain.

It resembled

The scratched slides of that yellowish green movie,

The ending of which

I caught once in the blink of my young eye

On the bulging TV screen of the set covered

With a knitted napkin;

A woman

In a supposedly green hat—you knew somehow, despite the black-and-whiteness of things—with a feather

Was kissed by a man—in a coat—

                                with a lost, rainy face.

Pick You Up

When I picked you up I was happy

With the strange reflected happiness

Of a man whom I did not know

You neither

Or maybe you'd already met him

Once or even twice or maybe

He just yesterday sent you

                            a friend request on Facebook

Or maybe while I write,

In this very moment

You stammer out

Your apology

Having overturned his lunch in the student cafeteria

In any case

He will be picking you up here one day

Most likely very soon

Sooner than you anticipate

The same way I do

Parking the car

In front of your lucky door

After the blind, stumbling rain

Under that rainbow

Fading away, trembling in the air,

Dwindling and reappearing.

Beads

Among the things that you forgot

Was the long string of white beads

Reminding me of rice—

I heard them tinkling in the bottom of the bag

Where your stockings and undergarments

                                      were stuffed.

I took all out

And saw the beads shining in the sun

In the shadow of my open trunk,

The passing and unneeded memento

Of your short Texan life.

Arts

They lived very happily

And by the end of their lives

They'd achieved the highest level

Of elegant dexterity

In the modest casual American arts

Of barbecuing and tailgating,

Football-loving, Zero-Coke-drinking,

French-fry-eating,

DUI,

Running with a pedometer,

Fitness, yoga,

And preserving their health and hearts.

El Paso

Tomorrow calls for wind in El Paso.
The red sand goes through the streets
Of the stone houses
And the cardboard houses;
The doors are closed,
As well as the windows.
The cactus
Is whipped with a spurt of a sandy wind,
And protrudes like an unshaven chin
Out of the white collar of white sand
With a black tie of black sand.

> "Is it really hot in El Paso?"
> "It is really hot in El Paso:
> You cry
> And your tears evaporate."

The windows are shuttered,

The shutters chatter,

But the window is unshuttered,

And the shutters do not chatter.

Lancaster

"The great-great-grandfather, a big lover

                          of Chardonnay and lobsters,

Came here on the steamboat a long time ago,

A big boss of a family full of uncles and nephews.

He founded Lancaster

Bank and Trust

That proudly stood on the outskirts of Houston.

The outskirts turned out to be the center.

The proud bank turned out to be modest.

The granddad turned out to be not as lucky

As his daring ancestor. He survived

The bankruptcy however

With the whole lot

Of his brothers, uncles, and nephews.

Only one cousin, the family legend says,

Was so depressed that he committed defenestration

Throwing himself out the twenty-sixth floor

Of a family building

But it is believed he was very timid,"

Announces the loud girl bartendress,

Extremely, in fact, loud,

Half of the bar can hear her.

She sighs and adds:

"I'm thirty-two, and pretty much done

With parties and drinking.

I don't like Houston,

But it's not Houston,

It's me.

I attend school—

Community college.

Next year I'm going to study

                        at the University of Houston;

They have grants, you know."

She rearranges the glasses and bottles,

And then again she is thunderously loud:

"On the next street you still can see

(Right here, the next turn)

The brick building

Pretty much lost between these new mirrors

That pass themselves off as buildings.

It has on its wall

The worn-out letters

That form the modest and proud name:

Lancaster."

ID

I wanted to pierce my brow

But I hadn't my ID

I told them: Hey

It's my body and I can do with it

Whatever I want.

That's exactly the point,

They replied,

We have to make sure this body

Is actually yours.

What Time Is It?

What time is it? Is it two thousand thirteen,

        or what is it?

A time of Skype conversations,

A time of the slowly growing cactus near the door;

A time of a child quickly changing,

A time of drawing fire trucks;

Public debates in Congress on TV, news from Russia;

A time of reading, walking,

A time of ouroboros, emblematic dialog,

        quickly turning

Everything into an unsolvable puzzle.

What a wondrous time—

Breathed over with fame,

Passing, eternal;

A time raving, prolific,

Miserable, pathetic,

Never returning.

Coca-Cola

This Coca-Cola tastes bitter.

While the sun is shining on the street

In the middle of December,

I look through the glass wall to the cars

Sliding down the street

Looking like multicolored bugs

Or else like a movie, muffled by the glass.

I have no one to mourn.

And only the piano knows not what it mumbles.

A stranger sits and watches the street.

His legs are crossed,

Arm rests on a newspaper,

I cannot see his eyes,

Only the raven-silver glow of the long, black hair

And a semi-Asian profile.

Conditioners

Austin, Austin

What have you done?

I am frozen, frozen

When you, too, will be not more than

Agone

No less

I would like to reread

In a few minutes

The golden, dusty hours

That I spend in a library

Pretending to read.

Feel free

To freeze me, Austin, feel free.

Utopia

Words

Spiral in my mind

Each

Around its axis

They shamrock on the edges

And slowly darken in the evening.

They tremble in the air

Emitting

A light chaotic jingle.

The line of the road

In a controlled, fluid movement

Writes a parabola

Of a U-turn.

The utopia

Of a city

Fades on the dim horizon.

Whitman

I like to leave an open computer on the kitchen table
With a turn-on Whitman,
Excitedly and coolly unscrewing the circles
Of the galaxies coming closer and closer,
               hooking and grabbing one another,
Bound to crush, explode, turn into
               some black holes of vastness
That will hungrily eat themselves out
               and leave breathless
Prostrating on the divan or bed;

I like to leave him
Speaking
To himself without a listener,
Chilling in the kitchen in an open notebook,
Crossing, with the borrowed voice
               of a professional reader,
The membrane of the speakers.

I like the thought

That this voice was born

Inside of my computer,

In which my lines are dwelling, dormant,

Like goggle-eyed fish on the oozy pond bottom,

                                    in weeds of Google,

Gleaming slightly

With fins and scales,

Silently screaming.

I like to leave him

Murmuring ancient incantations,

In vain, trying in the course of his speech

                                      to resolve the secrets

Of the universe with its puzzles

                                      of metal fusion temperatures,

With its seas of methane and the deposits

                                      of molybdenum on different planets;

With its corpuscles and homeomerias,

That construct all objects;

And with those who construct

Corpuscles and homeomerias, in their turn—

Mainly Greeks, I think, probably white-bearded,

But it is also probable, that the black-bearded,

Anaxagoras, someone of the ilk, Aristotle,

Who sincerely loved

Never existed places:

Lesbos, Miletus, Pathos, something along those lines,

                              Stagira.

Let him try once again to reformulate

       the same questions: Why all the commotion?

Why all the confusion?

Where is the beginning and when

       should the end be expected?

Let him try to ruin and reconstruct our dearest,

       the most valued illusions,

Multiplying, progressing, widening, rising
Into the colonnades, palaces, highways, and alleys,
Obtaining the sensually perceivable,
Sufferable, prone to suffering bodies.

I like to leave him speaking
Until the battery dies and blacks it all out,
Leave him
Along with a washing machine
That seconds, supports, and pollutes
The sounds of well thought-over poetry
With the meaningless white noise;
And just go out
For a walk.

The Best Cigars

An old, striped hammock

Probably rotten

Hangs

Between a statue of the Buddha

And a small waterfall

That runs on batteries;

A horseshoe

Is nailed with rusting nails

Above the door.

Who could doubt,

Drying one's face and bare arms

With the terrycloth towel of heated air,

That this land,

Exhaustingly exotic,

Exists?

An ad for the best cigars

Above the dirty display window of the shop

Vaguely promises

Either a new life

Or the invention of a time machine

Not the type that takes you to the past,

But the one that allows you

To enter the scene of a black-and-white movie

                            from the twenties;

And, like any advertisement,

Is not

Entirely

Accurate.

Amanda

In a house with an old, creaky staircase

On the highest (the third) floor

Between light green walls

Hugging your brown bear during the night

You will spend one more year

Of your irrevocable youth

Among the books on the shelves

And the dusty bottles of nail polish

Of different elusively melusine colors,

And in my memory you will appear to be crowned

With a light that plays on your hair

Against the twilit window.

Odysseus

When Odysseus was leaving

With his crew of cutthroats

Dressed-to-kill pirates

Lucky merchandisers

Skillful swordsmen

For the unknown shores

Of North America

To disembark

In Miami

Where girls in bikinis

And cocktail dresses

With tanned legs and shoulders,

Golden down on their thin arms

Adorned with golden, jingling bracelets

Dance

When Odysseus left the bright shore

Of precious Ithaca

Of beloved Ellada

He did not anticipate

The future Hades

Of the insatiable Danaides of Hiroshima.

Naiads

Were waving their pale green arms

But Miami

Beckoned

The cheerful town

Sacrificed a bunch of cattle

Celebrating Odysseus's departure

With balloons, flowers, and flags

Women cried, dogs barked

Men frowned and laughed

All the boys hid

In the nooks between the barrels

On the ships called

Zorky, *Otvazhny*, and *Neustrashimy*

All the universe greeted Odysseus

When he sailed away

When he was back

After thirty-three years of his peregrination

When he was back

He was a white-bearded man

With wrinkled forehead

And eyes

Burnt by a laser ray

When he was back

Only one boy was waiting on the pier

An old space traveler himself

Clothespin

I have half of my childhood

Stuck in the era of black and white.

Devoid of color

Those pictures have deep shadows and

Dispersed soft light.

I, too, saw the red lamp in the darkroom

And the then-modern alchemy

Under whose magic on the paper

Our round laughing faces were becoming clearer

More decipherable every second.

Then they were hanging in the air

On a string across the room.

And my dreams in those times

Were black-and-white

Like television.

It

Was agreed among adults,

Those who dreamed in color

Had too-vivid imaginations

Rocking hazardously on the brink of disorder.

That's probably why

When I see my dead in a dream

I try to turn down the colors of their faces

They wither, become vaguer, more nebulous, cloudier

From one year to the other

As in a can with a reversing agent.

In the end

We all will be stuck

In the air of that nonexistent room

On the invisible string, secured by variegated clothespins

Losing one feature and then another

Until the paper is once again

Perfectly white, pure, empty.

The Communist Party of the Soviet Union

Yesterday at the state dinner

Clinton suggested everyone join the CPSU

Thoughtfully looking at the sunset

Throwing husks and peelings

                                    on the floor and then a lawn

While a saxophone growled.

A Variety of Dragons

Station

In the middle of that journey,

By the end of a winter day

Full of harsh wind, full of sharp fragments

Of disintegrated snowflakes,

We went under the roof

Of the place with the low ceiling,

Yellow because of the fumes

Of the oven, and the smoke of dozens

Of smokers who dined there.

Our unit train, the last train

To Petersburg

Was expected in twenty minutes.

We bought hot tea in chipped cups, and two sandwiches

In cellophane,

Chosen from among those

That looked less rotten.

On the station, the lonely, downcast lamppost

Was screeching under the wind,

The light was dull and did not

Break the thick, dark blanket

Of the evening, and the snow whirled.

The rails were glistening and vanishing

In several tens of meters.

The cracks in the window frames

Were approximately as wide as my finger.

If we are ever back to

This station in the snowy night,

If we ever have

This cracked cold tile revisited,

The dream revised,

The snow rebreathed,

The smoke respired,

The lamppost re-breaking the heart,

I will know then

That death could be re-deathed,

The born already could be reborn,

Life—relived,

Love—re-loved,

Child—delivered,

And the earth and the thought

Revolved.

Moscow

When I stepped onto the first threshold,

I turned around.

On the street the air was dim with smoke.

It seemed the low clouds

And the breaths of cars, factories

Interflowed into the evaporation of a creature

The many muzzles clenching their jaws

Through rows of teeth the pink, long,

Split, bisected tongues

Coiled and wriggled.

In the vapor,

The dark figures of the people moved, gleamed.

Under the spilled roof

Flashed the red traffic light,

And then a green light,

Like the round eye of a dragon.

When I stepped onto the second threshold,

I turned around.

In the room,

The marble shelves contained

Tall black volumes

Of *Moscow News*, *The Times*, *The New Yorker*,

Some of them partially translated,

Scanned, digitized, and now meant

To be thrown out,

But the owner probably hesitated.

Cobweb, cobweb

Covered all the corners, but in the left one

Under a dark plank that still had a trace

Of some painting—

An indiscernible but clearly Biblical portrait—

Stood a desk, a wide rectangular table

Piled with papers. A computer glimmered,

Papers blued and blinked.

The dusty retort of the vase contained

Nothing

Except for the multiple thin, parallel lines

                               of a whitish deposit

On its sides bulging

Like a magnifying glass.

The vapor streamed into the open window,

Billowing the light curtains.

In the next room,

On the floor were scattered the shards

                               of the green and brown glass,

Former bottles.

On the doorknob,

She strangled herself with remarkable equanimity.

It's like that philosopher who is believed

                               to have interrupted his life

By voluntarily holding his breath,

I mean it is probably hard to strangle yourself

When you don't even have your body hanging down;

But then it was said delirium helped her.

In the windows there,

The golden cupolas were shining.

Poplar fluff was trapped between the double windows.

On the third threshold,

I turned not.

Tattoo

when I met my Russian love

I asked myself

why could he not be a Frenchman

smoking a pipe and in a green velvet jacket

why could he not be an Italian man

in sharp-pointed shoes and with a wide smile

why

could he not be an American,

a professor at the university

                          somewhere in Seattle, Washington

with round glasses

why should he be so slender and

have a tattoo on his bare arm?

there was no one to answer me,

except for a pedestrian

smoking a pipe in a green velvet jacket

his sleeves rolled

in his sharp-pointed shoes

a wide smile, round glasses

with a tattoo on his bare arm.

Hairdo

In the presence of a hunter

With a weapon in his hand,

And a green iridescent feather

In his velvet hat,

The wolves are hiding,

The lion is roaming away

To lay down

Under the moss-covered log.

When you came,

Half of my fears were gone,

But some of them

Are still hiding

In my high hairdo.

Sharp-beaked,

With snakey tails,

And forked tongues;

They protrude from

The smoothly brushed,

Glaringly done hair,

And

Hiss.

Scarf

The ground wind of a blizzard,

Like a white dragon,

Was biting the boots and squirming,

And was sending a cold wave

Under the coat, up to the back of the neck,

With the needlelike prickles of boiling snowflakes.

After the blizzard,

All was calm.

The snow had been falling steadily

For fifteen minutes more,

For half an hour,

For a day and a half,

For seven months of the winter;

For several winters,

Barely interrupted

With self-asserting springs,

The springs were inhabited

By the same wet, cold winds.

In the alley,

All the trees were standing

Like evening–morning watch,

Never changing,

Calmly enduring the rain,

The sun, rainbows

That were induced

By the street cleansing machines in the springs.

The trees lasted,

Full of snow that clearly

In black and white contrast

Represented

Their perfect composure and utmost resolve.

The brightly lit tram,

All-orange,

Was working its way

Through the thick, dense blueness

Of a street.

Between the two rows

Of trees

The tram

Lightheartedly chinked and tinkled,

It hissed, it rang,

Spreading its yellow light in a rapid brushed movement

Along the snowdrifts,

Reeling it in,

And equally quickly uncoiling;

The rails were glistening,

Waiting to be uncarved

By the renewed snow;

In the silver, shimmering moonlight

I happily readjusted

My itchy, unending scarf.

Kiev Kitchen

Every time a water spurt

Crushes itself in the metal sink

I remember the metal sink

In Aunt Hanna's kitchen,

And I think

It takes only one short movement

To lift a head

Out of the plates and cups

To catch an eyeful

Of cheerfully chirruping

Chirping and prattling

Chestnut Kiev

Through the window

Curtained with magenta-pink chintz.

Siberian Dream

A double-bladed paddle

With which a kayak is managed

Now lies on the beach pebbles

And glistens in the sun.

In a blue, puffy coat

Protecting from the harsh wind

He squints at the river

That is so bright it's almost

Painful to look at.

A pot is on fire

And black tea is boiled

The cigarette is in the corner of his mouth

The fishing float levitates in the liquid sun,

And there is nothing else to want.

Story

Under that red lampshade,

Our mother read

A red wonder of a story bent

In the form of a horseshoe.

Assignment

Our true country, my friend, has no forests.

No fields.

No lakes.

No places.

Our true country is fearless and rainless,

A sunless country.

Let us then calmly

Fail

Our assignment, difficult and gainless.

When your body is covered with dead black leaves

And a slug is making its slow way

                            down your forehead,

Sleepless

Singing

Will be my main sustenance,

But before that,

Let us try

Not to fail

Our unthinkable assignment.

My Aunt's Ear Clips

On my grandma's veranda,

With elongated windows

Around the table that was half won back

Out of captivity from the thorny, wild rose bush,

In the Ukrainian sultry night,

The young members of the family

Gathered—

My mom, her brothers and sisters.

The conversation held above the cups with tea

Was remarkably empty and happy,

With bursts of white-toothed laughter.

I badly wanted to have the ear clips that glistened

In the straw hair of my youngest aunt—

The plain plastic glitter;

I thought there was nothing

                                    more beautiful in the world,

Under the dark blue poplar trees

With silver linings,

Hushed in the light of the moon,

Outshined

By the bulb without a lampshade

That buzzed

In the small nocturnal orchestra of insects,

Which hummed around.

The big moth with triangular wings

Was the noisiest.

Oh, I thought there was nothing more precious,

And could never be,

And look how right I was.

The Lake

We should have gone with you

To the summer field with unnoticeable flowers—

Trefoil, chamomile, cornflower.

The field between debris

And the reconstruction

Of that white church on the shore of the lake,

Reconstruction led by a bearded priest

And a group of architects and painters,

Some of them with summer girlish faces.

They keep their brushes dry

And their heads covered with white handkerchiefs

That do not conceal their braids.

We should have been sitting

On the shore, in front of the silent mirror of the lake,

Which is so clear that in the eventide,

It melts with the cloudless sky

So that it feels—doesn't it,

Like sitting on the edge of the Earth

In front of a light blue abyss.

On the lake, frogs start their "ribbit" symphony

               in B-flat major, opus number twenty,

For the full orchestra

With the wind instruments—

Willow harps, strings, and percussion.

At twilight,

The cupolas look like spacecrafts,

Ready to start their voyage to other planets.

The wooden boats are chained

To the improvised mooring berth,

Namely, to the wooden fence.

Someone splashes in the water

Near the bushes

In the twinkling, fading light of the wave.

Silver laughter is scattered above the surface.

We should have been sitting there,

But we weren't and wouldn't be, because we couldn't.

Library

Who would pay me for the last flicker of the youth

Relentlessly wasted in a library

Like in a prison between bookshelves?

Sometimes I find that

I act under an impression

That I am deathless

That's what justifies anyway

The meticulous savouring of the dust,

The goalless crawling

In an invisible glass jar

While in the sky a non-existing shepherd

Or better yet a cowboy

Whips sheepishly drifting clouds

With a twisted string of a wind.

Who would pay me for all the time wasted,

And in what kind of currency?

If only with glass beads,

If only with empty shells and rotten apples,

If only with stubs of pencils

Chewed by me while reading.

If only with all the precious stones in the universe

Which otherwise could have been never

Known:

A parallelogram of a table

Covered with a white fabric,

A branch of the pale purple lilacs

In a glass, magnifying the bubbles of air,

Sitting on the stalks;

In the crystal a beam is playing as a goldfish

Dispersing into a spectrum on a gray wall.

On the table there is a thin porcelain cup

With a tea trembling,

                catching a reverberation of the steps

Of a now dead poet, then a bolding dandy;

And a woman with a high hairdo in a white

Dress snuggles on a low sofa

Smoking a long gone cigarette,

Turning it all into an ash,

And then the picture darkens on the edges

                                        and starts burning,

The movie ends, a tape abruptly tears,

The nineteenth century reaches its destination,

Trains are on the tracks, the railroads

Smell pretty much like iron,

And, when I leave the library,

The clouds are different.

Incantation

During Russian nights I now

Speak another language,

Reciting

Verses out of the big, dark green volume

With letters distorted, unrecognizable;

Redirecting

The vectors of the winds

From the ones that turn the rusty weathervane

                                                to the southwest

To those

That turn this iron rooster

                                    with an arrow in its clawed grasp

To the northeast.

The tree gasped,

Brushed

Against the fleece.

The loud grackles stained the sky.

In the poor ceramic

I try to compose an impossible potion.

With the dignity of exasperation

I stubbornly try to convey

Russian thought,

Which is me,

That is wrestling in me,

Elusive, resilient, rebounding,

About the country

You could not care about,

In a tongue that those

Who care about the country

Never cared to know.

The willows are singing;

The wayward contralto

Is rolling

Down the marble staircase,

Until the quickly unraveling sound stumbles

Upon the end of the staircase,

And this is the end of the sound.

Cigarette

Under the door the stream of cold air,

Blue with cigarette smoke,

Was creeping.

In the middle of the night,

I went in my cheerful pink slippers

To the cold toilet

Where the water

Was murmuring in a rusty pipe.

A young woman in a hospital nightgown

    with a big hole revealing her round shoulder

Was gazing into the stopped eyes

        of her winter reflection

In the dark mirror of a window.

She was thoughtfully smoking a menthol cigarette

    with a golden ring on the filter,

Sculpturing a yellow dragon

In a nictitating lamp

Above her head.

She was lightly tapping her cigarette

                              with a habitual finger,

A free hand relaxedly lying

On her five- or six-month-old

Accurate belly.

An Ability to Speak

A day with a child

Who does not talk yet,

Is like a day with an old relative,

Who has already told the world

Everything the world might have wanted

To know:

Listen closely

For hours

To the needs of a creature

Who makes efforts

To express its unspoken desires,

Indescribable wants,

Undefinable urges.

The time and space of unanimity

Slowly, day by day,

Draw back, like the sea after a flood.

Everything restores itself,

Obtains

Forms,

Is explicitly and reiteratively

Defined and redefined

With the persistency of motherhood:

"Mama," "eat,"

"ball," "lamp," "cat."

Then a cat and a lamp,

Unnamed, come across his face,

Summoning his features into one or another

Kaleidoscopic combination.

Every morning

Awakening in the sunny room,

We used to forget

The names of things.

On exiting

Your early childhood,

Your tottering and babbling toddlerhood,

I slowly regain the sureness of my movements

And an ability to speak.

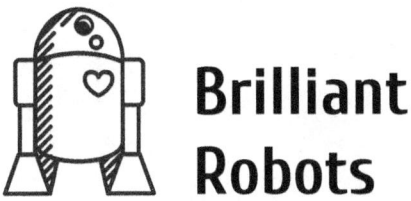

Brilliant Robots

Borges

According to Borges,

Mirrors are monstrous

But according to mirrors,

Borges is not reliable:

They have not reflected him

For quite some time now.

Limbo

Saint Electrocutor

Preached God to a small group

Of reverent fish

Fervent birds

They stood in the darkness

Under the big umbrella,

Wings and fins bristling,

Beaks and mouths agape in front of his arms akimbo

Frightened to the core of their small animalistic souls

Of the inevitable forthcoming limbo.

After the Rain

after the prolific rain

the pavement

was irreparably wet

a brilliant robot

was gliding along the street,

his red signals

duplicated by the reflection

I have all questions solved

except for the last puzzle:

why do you always have dry lips?

Buddha

Rotating the swishing short blade

In its long, skillful fingers

A dead-faced statue of the Buddha

Left a curvy roof of the pagoda

Under which it spent thirty-three years,

And went into the thickening darkness

Down the hill

Towards the glimmering lights

Of a virginal city.

Home

As a hermit crab

I leave my previous phone today,

And will be living in the new one.

Lipstick

a gruesome lipstick

nonchalantly applied

constructed

her sorrow of a mouth

Sect

an innocent insect

the member of a sect

of fliers on light

flies on the light

of my detached touchscreen

(phosphorescing in the night)

in full accordance

with the rules of the sect,

an invidious insect.

Machaon

moloch of my

mailbox

a rotating

chaos

a transparent

machaon

emerges

and dies,

wings lie prostrate

Count Leo Tolstoy's Estate

Count Leo Tolstoy's estate in Texas

A great aesthete

So eccentric

With whole baskets of blueberries

Cheerful maidens sing,

Going out of the forest,

Here they are

Between the trees

They are seen,

And you can also hear

The whistle of a train approaching a remote station.

How your boots shine

They are like a black sun

A Purple and Gray Umbrella

Today it is going to rain

Unless it is not going to rain

In which case

I am not going to take

A purple and gray

Umbrella

Unless it is going to rain

In which case I am going to take

The purple and gray

Umbrella,

But it's unlikely that it is going to rain.

1941

I nearly died

In '41

During the bombing of

Manhattan.

Porn

popcorn of scornful porn

on the screen

venomous

scorpion

reels

and stings

mama, I don't want to watch porno

anymore

no thanks, I don't read Theodor Adorno

anymore

Ataraxy

A vice-vixen breathed in all the oxygen

In the galaxy

Achieved the ultimate ataraxy

In every possible way

Thinkable for a foxlike creature

                             that outfoxed its foxiness;

It lies supine under the black skies

                             of the rotating galaxy

The galaxy rotates

Who cares about galaxies

The vice-vixen achieved the final ataraxy.

Landscape

kafkaesque

landscape

leviathan's realm

a daydreamer in a car

pierces a vista like a shriek

I wish I had not marred

the bloody windshield

slipping from nothingness

into obscurity

of harlequin harlem

ahnenerbe eden

Smoker

He smoked the whole pack of gasps and breaths

In a few series of short respites,

Then he went alone in the starry night

To buy a new pack of breaths and gasps.

Pretext

Under the pretext

Of descending into the garden,

Drinking the evening air

And counting the moons

He descended into the garden,

Drank the air and dew

And counted the moons.

Shih Tzu

her shih tzu

was a fierce fuzz of a thing

with a fake-Nietzsche mustache

9/11

I haven't seen her since pre 9/11.

I was so glad to see her.

She was in good shape, a good girl.

I am sure we will meet soon.

Ghost of a Bicycle

The ghost of a bicycle

Trails through the empty summer night streets

Where all the stores are closed,

The metal shutters and the locks

Are jingling

In the warm wind

Which dishevels the hairs

Of the silvery-blue trees.

The rusty chain of a ghost bicycle is loosened,

Its squeaking wheels are bent,

The leather seat is worn-out and cracked,

And the springs are grasped by corrosion;

In the glove compartment,

A monkey wrench dully clunks.

This is a wonder, but

The skull of a mockingbird

Is not broken yet

In the glove compartment.

Nothing but a tremble

Goes through the empty streets.

It will go through you

Like a nameless vibration

Slightly

Ringing

Through your bones

With its rambling handlebar.

The moonlight spokes

Will pierce your muscles with a spasmodic contraction

Of the eternal love

And ever-present pity

Of the full understanding

And explicit forgiveness,

For one short moment

Before it strolls

Down the hill

Forever,

Pulling along

The sonorous dolor

Of its nonexistence:

The bell dinging,

The red rhombus of engraving: *Aist*

Glistening in the moonlight,

And a screeching lamp

Flashing

A sort of

Farewell.

Untitled

the bare and pure

branches

purloin

in the sky

bare and pure

porcelain

pomegranate

gossamer

in the eye

on the lashes

Cat

A cat diligently casts

A convoluted shadow

Shaped like a cat

(Significantly changed

Prolonged

And oblong),

A shadow like an abstract twisted cat,

An essence of a cat,

A catnessence itself.

R705QS

I've been living

In this bivouac

For nearly two years now,

With no one around but my faithful

R705QS.

Or I should say, we've been living.

When our spacecraft

Emitted the last long cry

That most probably was lost

In vast space,

I still had hope, and so my faithful

R705QS

But the sand kept creeping slowly into its mechanisms,

It lost the velocity of its left manipulator

And the lower jar jammed in its joints.

R705QS

Will have a record of our misadventures

When you'll discover it one day.

I should now turn it off

It quickly runs out

Of its leaking battery,

And in about two weeks

The nine-month-long night starts.

Farewell

I am stuck in a cosmos vacuum

Like an amoebic vacuole

The cord that connected me to the ship is broken

Irreparably

Like the cord of a mother

And drawing an imaginary parabola

Slightly rotating

I slide adrift down the abysmal night.

How far my travel will be,

You could not imagine, nor I,

The transmitter is broken

But I still have air,

Probably too much of it.

Please decode this fainting signal

Tell them I died for the fame of my native planet,

In the name of the Emperor,

And for those I loved.

 **Apocalypse of Suburbia**

Undo

Unflake the snow,

Unbloom the flower,

Unknow the name,

Unburst the bubble.

Unsee the seen,

Unhear the heard,

Unleash the dog,

Believe in God.

Buoy

In the colorful small town on the Italian Riviera

An adopted girl

Usually spent her summer

Outrageously bored.

She suffered from diabetes.

"My stepmother is dear,"

She said, the sun was slicing her puff body

Through the striped green-white tent.

"And she has so much jewelry

And make-up

That her drawers are about to snap.

My stepfather nags but he is intelligent,"

She added yawning,

"He is very clever, you know."

On the sea balanced a red boat or maybe a buoy

Since the day was shiny

And the sea was bright blue

And the red was floating

It was hard to tell.

Preferences

I prefer my train to be not so punctual

My eggs not hard-boiled

My friends not very attached

I prefer my book interrupted

My books aslant

I actually prefer my phone not fully charged

My bag unzipped

My hair undone

My watch forgotten

I prefer my poems unrhymed and lying,

And preferences undisclosed.

Wife

I am still astounded that I am a woman
one can say, it's about time to get used to it
or at least I could have married a girl
(preferably Mary)
so that she could be a writer's wife.

A Great Shot

I saw her

In a blatantly short dress

With tiny buttons and flowers

White-haired blue-eyed pink-mouthed

A pearly, naughty mouse

On a train from Oxford to London

I had my Canon on

I silenced the sound

Gently pressed the button

Diaphragm set its blades ajar

Shrunk with a clang—

The floral mechanics of a predator's petals—

And went wide open.

She heard the sound

She saw the glitter of the lens

I caught it

As I caught her wisely smiling.

A Photo Not Taken

No flash

Will cut it all out of the darkness.

I should simply memorize it.

A wind dashes

Into the bushes,

Or maybe it's a raccoon.

I'm glad to hear you,

Night city's resounding basso profundo,

Glorious legato of a warm air,

Delivering a remote, wordless song,

Floating into the open window,

Slowly jingling in the room.

I'm standing in front of the cadence

That quivers in the air,

And scatters

And shatters into the inaudible,

Slips into the unheard.

I am just a photographer

Who takes no picture;

Am a sincere friend

Of all things silenced,

Of all things muted,

Of all things hurt.

Thing

Not once

I dropped this thing,

It stings me.

I keep it in my pocket,

I warm it on my lap,

I wear it in my bag.

I feed it like a mouse

Through the needles of its teeth.

I look in it, like I have never looked

Into the opaque nickel of a mirror,

And it—

It stings me.

I should shut it down,

And let its wicked battery run dry.

Neck

I slowly grew aware

Of the fact that you have shoulders,

That you have a neck,

That you are real,

That you are not just a computer program

Designed to

Make me feel

That you are real,

That you have a neck.

Photo

In that photo

I like your lips the most.

Your eyes are stern,

But I like the lips.

I opened the picture on my computer to look

A little closer;

The image is grainy.

Your lips have this curve,

I caught a glimpse

Of it watching some old western

About Texas,

Or Tennessee;

The pixels are like paint dabs;

Your lips could be seen,

And I think that they had been seen

By me

In Tretyakovka, Uffizi, del Prado,

Or in the London

Gallery.

This is easy:

When I zoom out the picture,

I will surely see

A shiny metal helmet

Of a cuirassier.

Fountain

The crystals drip in this fountain for days and days,

The surface covered with dead leaves and petals

From the nearest bushes of English roses.

A little further, beyond the gate,

The spiral highways coincide, bifurcate, and wreath,

The streams of cars flow freely and interlace;

Here is a grackle drinking the basilica and skyscraper

From the stone bowl.

The wind is warm,

It goes through the desert and the border,

It transports a palm of ideal, octagonal,

                                        red sand grains,

The plastic cup stolen from a coffee shop,

A check,

A cigarette stub,

A paper scrap, a hair wisp,

And a sound of gasp,

Not necessarily in that order.

Waterfall

Hiding under the rock, almost unseen,

Dispersing the ray in the air,

                        the small waterfall whirrs,

The swoosh of the bluest silk,

                flowing and swirling and folding.

In this pond, lives a moss-backed turtle.

The lantern staggers, while I drink coffee substitute,

The glass throws on the tablecloth

                the quivering reddish reflexes.

The most eloquent tree in the park

                        is irritated and muted,

It suffers from a sudden severe case

                        of arboreal dyslexia.

San Antonio

When the rain rushed,

We ran under the tent.

The rain stained

The white fabric napkins,

Forgotten on the tables.

The iron chairs

Quickly were glistening.

On the leaves of succulent plants

The rain swiftly threw bum-bum-bum put-put-put.

The surface of orange juice in the high glass

Mottled in dozens of puny explosions;

Orange turned opaque.

In the twinkling,

The street emptied.

The iron gates of the garden

Were left without supervision,

Ajar,

Swinging

Back and forth against each other.

Someone's bicycle,

Leaned on the wall,

Fell down with a rattle;

The bell meekly jangled.

Order

He is sitting in San Antonio

Playing computer games

All night long and also during the whole day

Having dropped out

Of pharmacology at UT

Every now and then

Doodling the characters

Of his favorite computer games

Does he even regret anything no he doesn't

His life is magnificently adjusted

To all his needs

Every day I see his photos in the stream

They are always the same

But what is out of common order

Is that he posts from time to time pictures

                              of a red-breasted robin.

But now this, too, is order.

Map

a map of a summer day spent on the veranda
without regret, from an open hand the day slips out,
                                        here it is, it's finished
with the disappearing scent of dust or that of lavender,
I don't distinguish

everything is soaked in summer merriment,
                                    short, omnipotent, ubiquitous.
on the table is a map, a glistening compass,
                                          a dragon-tailed kite;
and the annoying whining of a duet of mosquitoes
revives the aerial denseness of the night

Apocalypse of Suburbia

Why, the road does look like a mirror.

I don't

Accelerate,

Gliding like a gondola

Between the narrow concrete shores,

Only a little—four miles an hour—

Over the speed limit.

The void landscape

Will meet us as soon as we are out of town.

The rain spurts

Together with the windshield wipers

Are ruining

The images of the pickup trucks

And wagons.

I misconstrue the cars,

Glowing in the blurred lights of traffic

Like emeralds and rubies.

Your face is cherubic,

Accurate apocalypse of suburbia.

A Unicorn, a Dandelion, and a Lion

They sniff with their snouts

The Galateia vacancy,

They open their pink jaws,

Reconfiguring their muzzles

Into the vague resemblance of a smile,

A unicorn, a dandelion,

And a lion.

Cleaning up the claws

And readying the teeth

To tear the untearable up,

A unicorn, a dandelion, and a lion.

Their eyes are blue

Their eyes are violet

They are looking at you

With the expression

Of bearing no expression,

A unicorn, a dandelion, and a lion.

 **Self-Loading Parrots**

Shield

your shining shield protected me from the arrows
that were pouring down on me, and when a bird
was crying
standing on an eyeless skull
your shining shield reflected the green sparkle
of its black wing

when I woke up
I still had your umbrella
standing near the door

Marketplace

At the mart, at the cheerful market,
Where the melons are steeply-sided and are so yellow
That they are almost pink,
There are also aubergines, deeply violet,
So dense and steady, that you can in fact touch them.

The peaches sit together like eggs in a nest
In big, wooden, parallelogram boxes;
The fruits are downy and firm—
They ought to be just fine in a few days.

There is a corner where they sell rotten cherries.
They sell the shuddering shadows of flowers,
The snow of the past several years,
And the porous skin of tangerines,
Under a bright, explicit advertisement:
Don't Buy This,
In the cheerful market.

An idle meanderer, in the ridiculous clothes

                                      of a blackbird,

With a white beaked mask on his face—

In his spacious pockets something tinkles,

Let's say, the bottles with elixirs,

Sharp metal instruments, and the key of his Phaeton—

Frequents the store.

He meticulously chooses, paying attention

To details that escape the seller himself:

To winds that change their direction,

To the order of the birds in a flock flying

                                      above the tower,

To the order of the freckles

                        on the cheeks and nose of a girl

Who buys one fragile, pale flower

Out of the rich family of Violaceae.

He picks up a transparent feather.

Pendulum

The clock is ruined,

The pendulum is long stuck and corroded.

The mirror amalgam,

Alloy of mercury and silver,

Has deteriorated wondrously.

A lacey skeleton,

I like your interstices,

And a netlike sack of the ribs.

It is a pity;

Where

Did you lose the liquid lithium of your sky-blue eyes?

Your wig is covered

With fine, pinkish, powdery dust

That settled

A worn-out while ago,

At the time of those

Long-gone shimmering dresses—

Threads made by silkworms—

That smoothly swooshed along the marble floor.

Letter

While he was writing an old-fashioned letter

He noticed that the closer to the end he was

The stranger were things happening at the beginning

Of the page—it withered, twisted, curled,

                                       and finally a city

Was burning on the horizon

Black chains of smoke enclosed the sky

And when he'd finished his letter

The beginning was a trace of soot

Dispersed on the table.

Room

> *Enter Servant, and two Murderers*
> *Macbeth*, Shakespeare

When the servant enters,

The room is empty.

On the table is a plate,

On the plate is a lonely apple,

And a pit of a plum still glistens.

A fly buzzes annoyingly.

The heavy curtains

Barely allow a slanted ray

To stain the floor,

The table,

The plate.

Dream

I dreamt or dream, for I saw or see you

Measuring the space of your house

With a stride,

Seemingly determined,

But in fact meandering;

Casting your gaze out of the window

Where all the small paths and big roads are well-known

Since the autumn, winter, spring

Schooldays;

Auburn, burnt, autumnal,

Windowless, wailing, wintry,

Simmering, spinning, summery, mesmerizing—

The paths of your works and days;

You should stop now and pour I think

Into a low glass

Some reddish-amber liquid—liquor?

What is it?

I could not see.

Whiskey?

A red cat with red whiskers

Might as well purr and rattle

Like a red toy tractor

From the cozy nook of a flat.

Here they come, the aestival

Festivities:

The eating of poplar fluff

And the tasting of dust

Covering and coloring the swelling eyelids

I saw or I see

Lanes

Never crossed by me,

Buildings

Never visited by me,

Trees

Never spotted by me,

Sky

Never seen

Clouds

Never caught, never seen, never captured,

Being crushed on the edge of consciousness

Yet never really being crushed,

Just like you were

Never seen, never heard, never enraptured,

Being crushed on the edge of consciousness

But never being crushed

Rays,

Never refracted by my

Lenses,

Lights,

Never reflected in my eyes.

Fish

Fish cried silently in the depth of the pond.

So silently

It almost did not cry

At all.

Only

The oblong tear reverberated

                              as the fish dragged it along

And another tear like a muted bell under the water,

                              after the first one

And another one after the first two

And some more

Streaming like pearls

On an invisible string

As the fish dragged them along and cried and sniffed

Ding-ding-dingledy-ding

Falling

What a rabbit hole, at times tight and narrow,

At times wide like the gate of a marble palace.

A jam jar was left on the table with its lid ajar.

At times walls are dark, at times they shine

                        with an eye-hurting luster.

The stretching *musculus temporalis*

Shuts the mollusc

Of a jaw.

The milk is spilt, and the apple split in two,

The wine grapes are rotten,

But you could tell

That she was falling

And falling

And falling

And she was falling

And yet she never,

She never fell.

Letters to Several Personages.
To Mr. Christopher Brooke

Don't grieve yourself with my grief,

    do not mourn my non-existing sorrows.

I, too, have something I can feed my idleness with.

I know no sadness, I have my share of amusement

Portraying grackles all day long, comparing leaves.

The squeak and crunch of birds,

        poor little mechanisms,

Euphonize my finite hours,

      in ethereal voidness spent.

The ringing chain of blunt events

Makes its stubborn life through me

By means of reproducing sounds.

All that I ever saw and did—no more, no less—

Makes me cast this occasional glance

On the low sun,

Unhindered by the interweaved branches of trees.

I stare through the charcoal feather, stopping
Exactly where the road slightly bends.

I know I have a listener in you,
You have enough compassion and patience
To pay attention
How they click and clack,
The milky, opalescent, quartz, monotonous beads
In my infinite rosary; thus, I had
Almost everything that one could only have
In this dolorous vale.

So, how could I lament? No, I have no complaint.
The only duty that I struggle with
Is to code into the pure, clear, and decipherable lines
My blurry, iridescent, muddy tears.

Whatever you derive from it, please do;

That's what you should have done.

I have no wishes except for those you wish.

My modest gift to you is this

Scarce, imprecise translation from John Donne,

From English into I don't know which

Language.

Wriggle

a bicycle gleamed like vinyl

like Vermeer

the wheel wriggled and veered

reeled on the sand

leaving a queer squiggle

Stanzas

It hurt your ears to hear it.

Perhaps there's still a soul;

A place without a place.

A place without a palace,

A place without appearance

Where purity is rooted,

Integrity is planted,

Where everything is soiled,

Where everything is spoiled.

The only home is QWERTY,

Appeasing and well-known.

And with your limits strained,

And with your thoughts afoul,

And with your memories stranded,

And with your fruits befouled,

You know as good as QWERTY,
The Lord is full of mercy;
The Lord is full of mercy,
And so there is no soul.

It hurt the objects fleeting,
It hurt the objects seen,
It hurt my fingers tapping.
It hurt my eyes to see
And I was dull and bored.

It could have hurt a daemon,
A seraph, and a man.
It could have hurt a woman.
It could have hurt the Lord.
It could have hurt the Lord,
And yet he was not hurt;
The Lord is full of wisdom,
And so there is no Lord.

Phantasm of a Bicycle

Through the tiny peephole

Of a heavy door

The summer day,

Muddy and blurry,

Shone

With a phantasm of a bicycle

Dwelling at the bottom of it

Like a long, silver fish gleaming

                            in a too-narrow channel.

Robotic Paradise

The mechanical garden of early paradise

Is inhabited by self-loading parrots

And automatic monkeys,

Chirping on trees with bronze leaves,

Which drop heavily,

With a cling,

On a platform.

The branches are burdened

With bitter fruits

In stranded petals,

And cling to the earth

Which is covered with a white deposit

And corrupt mushrooms.

In the early garden,

Thick as forest,

Forgetfulness is reinstalled.

A learned alchemist, trigonometrician, and botanist

Fuses a violet in a retort,

Not noticing that the soot

Mars the map on the oak,

As well as the delineation of the human body,

Inscribed in a circle

Inscribed in a square.

It is impossible to leave the forest

Of easily achieved

Automatic self-satisfaction;

The lair of a beast,

The palace of a vestal

Virgin.

The clear sight of a hermit

Is distorted by his prismatic lenses.

The cymbals and drums

Clack and chime:

A kind of golem orchestrates

The march of robotic existence,

The dance of mechanical creatures.

Bird

A bird with a crimson chest
Sings
In a high, thin-wired cage.

The plumage of its lyre-divided tail
Pours down on the dirty floor
Between the bars,
A redundant abundance
Of violet and turquoise feathers.

Iron rods ring like iron rays.
The pea-green bird's thin throat
Vibrates while the song breaks away.

On its sharp yellow beak the thin-bladed nostrils
Tremble when it sniffs the almond flavor of cyanide,

It wears a beak as if

It were a crooked nose of an evil mask

Covering the small face

Up to the squinty, fulgent eyes.

I feed the creature

With meaty, lush fruits,

Citruses

That pulsate when I slice them

With a narrow, rusty knife.

At four in the morning

It stops its vocals for half an hour

I lie down on the hard wooden bench

To have a short, restless respite.

I do not change my dress,

Do not fix the holes in the elbows.

The black wings of my bird

Flutter chaotically,

Its claws squeeze the twig in the cage,

Leaving cuts

From which violet blood spurts

And dries all over.

I am offered emeralds for my bird, rubies,

But I laugh,

I laugh,

Covering my mouth

With my hand, because

In my upper jaw

Two front teeth are missing.

Oh the untiringly soloing bird

Sings from dawn to dusk

And from dusk to down

In my poor, empty room,

Where the flakes of paper,

A slew of dust, hair, and fluff

Roll from one corner to another

And then back again

With a mass of mice.

I don't move

The heavy curtains

On my tall windows,

And the cold wind swishing in the crevices

Does not bother me a bit.

A Visitor

Islington, Camden, Kensington,

Cambridge, Oxford, and Somerset,

Salisbury, half a dozen hamlets

In an achronological sequence

Of interrupted geography,

In all the red-bricked, chess-squared grotesquery,

Were summoned at once

By some sharp-beaked pedestrian

In a mask,

With dry rose sachets

In his pockets,

A well-known herald of inescapable death,

Later on, in the distorted memory of

Descendants—

A bronze equestrian subjugator,

Some medieval sadist,

Some terrible wreck,

Thrust the patinated spurs

Into the warm, bronze abdomen,

Squeezed with his crooked legs

The breathing, bronze, soft thorax.

Ribs

Every time now I have something written

I hope and I fear, this is all.

These raving days however

Not even a neighborhood passes

Before I must cry again.

I do not even know

Should I despair, or should I despair.

Through the habitual English

You can feel the ribs of hidden unknown Russian

As through the dress of your woman

You can feel my ribs.

Difference

And even if I'm in love.

What difference does it make?

The sun was not warm today

But the moon was full.

Words

Are you aware

Your words

Mess around

Rotate by themselves

After you probably

Have forgotten them.

They are barbed and whiskered;

I unhook them from my hem and lining.

Yesterday I was bitten

By the one

Hiding in my pocket.

In the morning

I discovered one entangled

In my hair,

And it was

Blinking.

Insomniac

You are coming at night,

And your body is ringing,

What do you do there?

Why are you giggling,

Why are you staring

Into the ceiling,

Eyes like two radiant lights.

Why can't you sleep?

It's too light to sleep

With your eyes like two lamps,

Open like that.

Shut those lids,

Let me rest.

Gmail

Gmail

Informs me:

"You are invisible."

At least I know now.

"Go visible,"

It offers.

Thanks Gmail.

Shorter

When I want to write to you, "My dear, dear,"

When I want to cry to you,

                      "How will we live now, tell me!"

When I want to whisper to you,

"When will you kiss me? Will you be gentle?"

I catch my hand in the air,

Oh I know what to do,

I always have a light-feathered word in my sleeve

In a pocket, or behind my ear,

Sharp-pointed word behind the sharp-pointed ear,

And I always

May throw at you, "Thank you,"

Or, simply, "No."

"No"

Is better. Much better. Much better.

Breathe deeper.

Shorter.

Message

I received your electronic message.

It was very precious,

Especially the passage

Where you said you write with your mouth

Tied, but you asked me at least to leave your hands

Free;

But I liked the most the fact

That it was thoughtfully divided

And the passages were numbered,

And that you respect my husband,

And that you regard my calmness

With due

Esteem.

I think I might have received it

On Wednesday, and my maid Glasha

Had it saved and printed,

But I might just as well have collected it

From a tin post box

Written on real paper;

The red and blue alternating stripes on the envelope

And the curious postage marks:

One of them with the photo of Budapest,

And another one with a portrait of Rosa Luxemburg;

I might also have taken it

Out of the hands of a wearily frowning stranger,

The scroll perhaps,

With a stamp on it and

The coat of arms

Identifying the sender:

The left supporter is a lion,

The right supporter is a griffon,

The shield is blue,

In the helmet

Snakes are twisting and sizzling.

I have decided

I had better run today,

Since I decided

To run daily or maybe

Not daily but at least weekly.

The boat

Jangles meekly

On the shore;

I've discovered, however,

That I am too lazy to run;

So it all relapses

Into long walks

With long stops,

But today

It is acceptable to make an exception;

I will run then.

...I was lying on the planks,

Traveling

With my sight

Back and forth

Along the gnarls, rings

And knots,

The growth

Of grass;

Along the

Never stopping surface of the stream—

Water

Melting and fusing,

Fusing and melting—

When I accidentally

Dropped your message,

Though it was precious;

It blobbed and drowned

Making no sound.

Hotel Room

The hotel room

Will never tell you

Its story.

The mirror does not really

Reflect the guest.

It's seen so many

That it does not notice you

And shows

You slower than you move.

The bed has lost its memory.

No one's kissed

A man or a woman.

And even if

A murder had happened,

Stains of blood

Were on the floor

And on the walls,

You would not know.

The same small button

Switching off the light

Which the murderer touched,

You touch.

You turn on

The water

Trying to wash off

The victim's DNA.

Evidence

The sea went gradually into the sky

And melted there.

I found the green stone.

The shore was full

Of evidence,

Of endless silent life,

Signs of ceaseless tectonic satisfaction

Of primordial hunger:

Shards of shells

A dead crab

The citations of the weeds

The feather of a gull

And an empty medieval can

With a still perceptible

Inscription

Coca-Cola.

Flip

The words of a foreign language

I don't feel them

Tasting as through cloth

Lemon is not sour

Sugar is not sweet

Honey is not viscous

Light is dim

Darkness has lights.

But you are attuned to them, reader

You fully grasp

Truly understand

Everything I might have meant

But did not.

About the Author

Vasilina Orlova was born in the village of Dunnai in the Russian Far East in 1979. She has lived in Vladivostok, Moscow, and London, and is now based in Austin, United States.

She holds a PhD in Philosophy and is the author of seven novels in Russian—among them *The Voice of Fine Stillness*, *The Wilderness*, and *The Supper of a Praying Mantis*. She has also published several books of prose and poetry, including *Yesterday*, *The Wilderness*, and *Quartet*.

She is the recipient of several Russian literary awards and is a laureate of the Anton Delvig Prize for the poetry book *Barefoot* (2008).

She has written in English since 2012, her first publication in the language being in *Di-Vêrsé-City*, the Austin International Poetry Festival anthology. Her poetry and prose has been translated into English, French, Spanish, Bulgarian, Ukrainian, and Russian.

The Lake, first published in the *Di-Vêrsé-City* anthology, 2013, is reproduced here with slight alterations.

www.ingramcontent.com/pod-product-compliance
Lightning Source LLC
Chambersburg PA
CBHW022358040426
42450CB00005B/234

* 9 7 8 0 9 9 1 6 0 0 9 0 8 *